Also by James Stack

World's Fair, a memoir

PLEASURES & SEASONS OF VERMONT

James Stack

Copyright © 2013 by James Stack

All rights reserved under International and Pan-American Copyright Conventions. No part of this publication may be reproduced, stored in or introduced into a retrieval system, or transmitted, in any form or by any means (electronic, mechanical, photocopying, recording or otherwise), without the prior written permission of the copyright owner of this book.

ISBN: 1481208152
ISBN-13: 978-1481208154

This book is a work of fiction.
Names, characters, places and incidents either are products of the author's imagination or are used fictitiously. Any resemblance to actual events or locales or persons, living or dead, is purely coincidental.

Cover photo credit: © Imagestate Media Partners Limited - Impact Photos / Alamy

For
*Alex, Beau, Junior, Lulu,
Pip, Sandy, Spot, Tippy &
Trek*

PLEASURES & SEASONS OF VERMONT

TABLE OF CONTENTS

The Pleasure of Vermont	5
Audubon Neighbors	7
Baby Birds	9
Black Bears	11
Blueberries	13
Bobcat	15
Butterflies in Love	17
Christmas Morning	18
Coyote	20
Darkness	22
Deer	24
Fall Apples	25
First Snow	27
A Stealth Fox	29
Green Mountains	30
Harvest	31
Hay	33
Hummingbirds	35

Ice Storms	37
Irene	39
Forests	41
Maple Sugar	42
Monarch Butterflies	43
Moose	44
Mud Season	45
Owls	47
Porcupine	48
Snowshoeing	51
Snowshoe Hare	53
Sunrise	55
Thunderstorms	57
Turkeys	60
Turtles	62
Seasons of Vermont	64
I. Winter	64
II. Sugaring	64
III. Mud	64

IV.	Spring	66
V.	Black Fly	67
VI.	Summer	69
VII.	Harvest	70
VIII.	Canning	71
IX.	Foliage	72
X.	T'aint Nothin'	74
Acknowledgements		75

THE PLEASURES OF VERMONT

My dog, Trek, and I relish
the countless pleasures that come
with living in Vermont. From awakening to the superlative
spring and summer sunrises and subtle morning hum,
through the joyous songs
of each glorious autumn day,
to the whistling
winter wind
bringing sleep, secure
in knowing our dazzling
canopy of stars will not fall.

Whether it is abundantly sunny with clear,
brilliant light, or it is a blinding blizzard
with howling winds and horizontal
snow, we are blessed to be situated
in surroundings of timeless beauty. We
live encircled by a perpetual state of grace
that others seek. Be these seekers the
autumn peepers, winter skiers
or summer vacationers, they are all in
search of the rapture
that composes our nature.

At times we may find ourselves
out of kilter, forgetting the kismet
we have here in Vermont. These unfortunate
episodes may be brought about by the
absence of loved ones, mistaken
communications, or merely
errors in judgement. As if
from a distance, we
see our fellow Vermonters as
being enclosed by a golden glow
of which we long
to be a part.

Unbeknownst to us, they see that we, too, are
within this sacred, golden radiance.
Presently we remember that
like all Vermonters, we are always
enveloped within this warm sphere,
this loving embrace.
We had simply forgot.

It is then that we most
appreciate being in Vermont.

It is at these times that I look at Trek
and smile. Trek, in turn, looks up at me and
returns my smile. And we continue on our journey.

Such are the simple pleasures of living in Vermont.

AUDUBON NEIGHBORS

The unassuming red clapboard farmhouse
at the junction of our road has
stood sterile through transient times. It
recently sold to a couple from
Florida, and now wildflowers and blueberry
bushes sprout where, centuries ago,
veggies developed and cows
browsed. The entrance across the yard,
previously the playground for old
broken implements, is now
imprinted with generous varieties of
annuals and perennials welcoming our new
neighbors home.

Initiating an introduction, my dog, Trek,
and I discover that they volunteer
for the Audubon Society. They
reside in Vermont from April thru November
to be conveniently on hand during
the visitation of the birds and butterflies.

Naturally, these same fauna journey south
during our cold months, some relaxing
in Florida with the other "snow birds." While
there they manifest a drab, gray
appearance, or so
our Audubon neighbors enlighten us.

Upon migrating north they morph
into their vibrant plumage. We
are advised this transformation aids
our feathered friends' regeneration
in the cycle of life.

On a night our new connections join
us for a casual dinner, they

oooh and aaah over all the
flying friends that flit about our
field. Of course, we are not insulted
that they do not react as
favorably to our meal, because *our*
delight is in watching *their* enchantment.

Like these animals that alter each year,
our neighbors' property is
transforming into a magnet:
One for others, the others for one another. As
Trek and I daily skirt their home, we
delight in this multiple metamorphosis.

Such are the pleasures of
Audubon neighbors summering in Vermont.

BABY BIRDS

While Vermont's various birds build
their sundry nests, my dog,
Trek, and I welcome the spring
with invigorated prepping of
our yard and garden – me with spade
and Trek with paw.

I.

Three blue-as-the-sky robin's eggs
crack, the babies grow, and
take an early flight, ending up
hip-a-de-hopping around the yard.
Four days these three go from
place-to-place scattering like
dandelion seeds until there are two:
One last seen on the window
ledge feeding as I watch
engrossed in the love shown by the
parents. The other finally reaches
the top of the picnic table
which is its last spot.
Fly away little robins.

II.

The ducklings count to five as they
swim around the pond, with
some displaying greater independence; ever so
tiny but making waves like speed boats, they
rush to their mother as we approach. From
a distance they are quite brave, gradually
moving further and further afield
with their parents never far afield.
Then one day there are none.

III.

Two baby barn swallows perch on a

spruce limb while their parents circle and
circle, grabbing food, and delivering it to
their waiting mouths. Soon they separate,
yet still close to one another with
each taking a turn. I look away, and when I have
an opportunity to glance back
they are gone.

How sustaining the world we live in: While
Trek and I care for the land, the birds
care and nurture their young until
they fly the coop; and we all renew the cycle.

Such are the pleasures delivered
by Vermont's baby birds.

BLACK BEARS

Cornering
a crook in the
road, my dog, Trek,
and I grasp a
passing
glance of a gigantic mass
as it swiftly dissolves into the summer shrubs. Its
bulk assumes sluggishness, yet its agility and ability
belie its size. Like a full moon – purportedly plump in its
orange orb initiating navigation through the night – the full
fur of the black bear bestows an immense impression.

Walking through the wet snow we watch for bulging brush
mounds; rocky ridges; or hollows within fallen logs –
anywhere bears might nap. Not being true hibernators,
if distracted, they can easily awaken from winter's
respite. With a recent thaw a sow arose with triplet
cubs; from afar we witness them scamper across our
road, through depleted fields and into dense woods.

Stopping to assess the strength and starkness of fresh
autumn claw serrations on a beech tree, they strike a
chord as if angled lines for sheet music. Taking note of
clatter from above, our hike becomes dramatically
discordant. Like storybook bears they find honey
harmonious. Yet as true omnivores they refrain not from
any tenor they find in their path, on which trail we tread.

Safely home with Trek asleep at my feet, a rambling
black blotch plods across our lower field diverting my
gaze. Even from a distance it appears menacing with
noticeably enormous dimensions. Yet quite shy,
they prefer wild, wooded areas. Still, I'm
thankful to have the window and distance
separating us from this incredibly
bulky, beautiful bear.

Such are the pleasures of
sighting Vermont's black bears.

BLUEBERRIES

Brown bare bush branches bloom in shades of jade,
with intoxicating pale floret sprays, all but
invisible as if playing hide-and-seek.
They oblige the potent bees that
look and locate and lug
their nectar home
and pollen to dissimilar varieties.

Late fall's pruning boosts
bounteous harvests; early spring's
augmentation of loam with acidic mulch
amplifies nourishment; summer's progressive
passing produces
medium to large berries
in tastes tangy, mild and sweet.

Bedroom and kitchen windows afford
clear observatories for my dog, Trek, as he
fixates on the birds feeding on our blueberries,
while cumulus clouds try to obscure the azure sky
with harmonizing cobalt undersides and coatings.

Outside, as I pick, Trek saunters nearby and
sniffs. He longs to know why the birds,
and I, make a fuss. Finding a fallen
few he snuffles and shifts them
with his nose. Finally, he
resolves to sample one,
and finds a fondness
for the indigo orbs.

Others cover maturing bushes with netting, but
we adore assisting the birds amass for their migration.

We don't mind sharing.

It is the leftovers we relish, selecting the dark
delectables to enhance muffins, pancakes
and pies; or storing fresh frozen for
winter enjoyment with friends.

Such are the perks and
pleasures of Vermont's blueberries.

BOBCAT

My dog, Trek's, yawn radiates a moan which
wakes me from a late afternoon
catnap. Through the slit of
one eyelid I effortlessly telescope through
the window into
tepid, overcast surroundings, the bulk of my
vision absorbing a nearby blue spruce.

Reflecting on our morning's
walk in the woods, and how it
amassed an appetite for some shuteye, I
visualize the tracks we discovered beside some
wetlands: Round footprints
belonging to a bobcat,
larger than an ordinary housecat's marks, but
mimicking the stalk-sit-stalk
of their friendlier cousin.

While bobcats are polygamous maters
they are solitary animals,
yet accompanying the larger marks were
smaller tracks; this female was instructing
her young on the art of survival.

Lacking a keen sense of smell, bobcats
pursue their prey at close
range, affording Trek and me the
optimism that we might come across
her and/or her victim; but today this stalking
was but a lesson, or else Trek and I
interrupted her pursuit with our own.

And there, absorbed in the blue spruce
outside my window,
I perceive those superior, climbing
bobcats. Yes, all the time

Trek and I were about, she and her
young could have been scrutinizing us, with
slits for eyes, as they napped in the
shade of a large limb.

Smiling at the prospect, I make a mental note to
look skyward the next time tracks disappear. Oh, to
have glimpsed her tawny, summer coat,
short bobbed tail, or distinctive ears.

Such are the pleasures of finding
bobcat tracks in Vermont.

BUTTERFLIES IN LOVE

My dog, Trek, sleeps soundly and I work
away diligently in my study
while outside a vibrantly sunny,
blue-bird day lengthens along.

As a couple I know breeze into my mind it
causes me to reflect on their
recent erratic behavior.

Distracting me as I look out my window
are two Monarch butterflies in love,
mounting as one upon an updraft
— fluttering, rotating, spinning, gyrating —
like an uncontrollable miniature
hot air balloon, then
— *poof* —
they are out of sight.

While trying to remember where I had
misplaced my reflection, these same two butterflies
suddenly reappear, one chasing the other
as they descend in circles back to the ground,
only to again disappear from view
into the grasses for, I would suspect, a restful repast.

Yes, these butterflies, like the couple who diverted
my thoughts, have their ups and downs
all the while dazzlingly inspiring one another.

Oh, many are the pleasures of Vermont.

CHRISTMAS MORNING

Never one to oversleep, my dog, Trek,
licks my face to eliminate the slumber, and I,
uncertain if it is yet morning or still the eve,
wish him a Merry Christmas.

Tentative through the dark without any hint of
dawn, we arrive at the mudroom unscathed. Upon
cracking the exit a crisp clean cold burst of
air, as if blown by frosty the snowman, seeps
through the threshold and brushes against my
cheeks. Trek is out in a flash and back nearly as quickly.

With an ever so slight lightening of the horizon
I'm aware of the time – so I prepare
Trek's Christmas morning banquet and
some hot cocoa for myself.

Sitting to sip and savor the silent seconds we
stare at the fog slowly lifting from the valley. Abruptly the
air comes alive and glitters as if filled with a billion
tiny fireflies, and decorating the snow cover are a
zillion sparkling diamonds; the trees emerge encased by a
thin coat of ice crystals, giving the impression of
having been festooned by fairies.

Not a breeze or cloud stirs,
as the final vestiges of fog vanish and
– *snap* –
life in Vermont sparkles.

The warmth from the sun as it waltzes across the
walls is a welcome partner; and
the fireplace, lit and crackling,
affords us comfort as I unwrap presents, and
Trek plays with his new chew toy.

Today all is well.

Blessed are the pleasures
of life in Vermont on
a brilliant Christmas morning.

COYOTE

The naked night is immersed with
moonlight slicing through
suspended, severe tree limbs. In unison
my dog, Trek, and I cringe
as we chance upon a
mysterious shape: A solid black cat
passing on our
left. As we begin the final descent of our trip
even Trek appears leery of an
ebony feline crossing our path.

Having been diverted, we are utterly
unaware of the
lone gray coyote. We screech
to a stop. The coyote's
advancing is arrested. Steadily
he circles. His silvery mane
reflects the piercing slivers
of moonlight. Tips of jet black
ears stand alert. We stare, eye-to-eye.
Without a care,
he leisurely rotates right,
his bushy tail hanging
low and slightly
swishing as he saunters away.

Coyotes mate for life, but this one
travels alone;
perhaps out hunting
for a family anxiously awaiting
dinner in the den. Both a scavenger
and predator – an
opportunistic omnivore – it
would not be long before he
finds delectable edibles. Perhaps we saved the
black cat to alarm others another night.

Innate predators, coyotes' characteristic, high-pitched
howl ending with a series of yips can be heard at
dawn and dusk. Some say they sound
like a woman screaming in pain.

Driving up our winding dirt driveway
my shoulders drop and
my grip relaxes as our home
– a safe harbor – comes into view.

Such are the pleasures of arriving home
after eyeing a coyote in Vermont.

DARKNESS

The Vermont night sky is a
consortium of glittering diamonds; a
carpet composed of constellations every child
can catalog. It's as if we are able to extend an arm
and fiddle with the sparklers as they flicker at our
caresses, reverberating like an acoustic resonator. These
twinklers delineate the Milky Way within which we are
waylaid with zillions of solar systems at our
fingertips waiting to be played like a harp.

Still, the evening sky is empty space; the stars
are too remote to illuminate. While city lights cast a
disruptive glow, like an encasing sphere, Vermont has few
such smothering distractions, for once the sun has set the
chill moves in and the dusk descends to vacuum out
the light, secreting a sprinkling of stardust.

The moon perpetually alters the night's equation.

When new it provides for pitched-tar evenings with
effervescent heavens. The autumn stillness conveys a
silky silence, while the winter flurries dull in
the dark. After the snow melts, the spring
delivers a rebellious resonance from the
peepers, pining for the engorged orb.

When full it elicits the illusion of an eclipse with gauze
filtered radiance; as snow covers the ground, it
shines intensely, reflecting riotous rays of
light; and in the summer the trees
provide shade from the smolder
of the intense brilliance.

On the darkest evenings
my dog, Trek, and I marvel at the
penetrable blackness in which we navigate,

as if on a distant planet gleaning newly found,
friendly life-forms guiding us safely home,
where, in the translucent light, Trek
and I beam at the memory.

Such are the pleasures of the
darkness of nights in Vermont.

DEER

In pairs prance or singly strut, deer delicately dance;
sensing the slightest resonance or strange society,
stare over shoulders; seize like soundless sculptures;
await the risk to pass, or need to scamper.

Winter we liberate and trim wild apple trees for feed.
Spring fawns with does freely frolic in fields. Delightful,
stylish stirrings, grace in escape, and bounding back
into the forest. It is especially satisfying knowing
my dog, Pip's, scent and my taps on the window
protect our tasty gardens.

Stationed like a centurion, an eight-point stag,
still and straight, attends his herd. High hunting
season, his antlers rendered for rutting, the requisition for
mating rights when a buck's absorption lies not in
personal safety but in survival of the species. Determined,
he accepts a new, shy doe into his world.

Beneath gauze filtered skies, the arctic air
stings our skin, and our breath creates lazy clouds.
Pip and I come upon clean tracks which
continuously crisscross the corridor, a crossword
puzzle. Cresting a rise, two young bucks, silent
statues, gaze back, tails raised, white undersides. An
eternity within seconds, we regard their elegance,
they twitch, then vanish.

Such are the pleasures of
our dear deer in Vermont.

FALL APPLES

Apples are a special treat
for my dog, Trek.
Finding one he will ravish
its delectable sweetness
metamorphosing into a Cheshire dog
– smiling serenely.

Walk down any Vermont road,
dirt or paved, and
you're bound to find apple trees.
Some are from old orchards while
most are from seeds deposited,
as the majority of seeds are,
randomly.
These are Vermont's
wild apple trees
whose nectar varies from
haphazard cross-pollination.

Trek samples the different
wild varieties revealing some as
sensationally delightful. Others,
after tasting, he passes by.

Like Vermont's fall apples,
we encounter life's experiences
finding some good, some not so good, and
some, well, not good at all.
Just as we crawl before testing our legs, and
through the falling we gain knowledge,
we try again, and move on to something new.

Like Vermont's fall apples, we keep
experimenting. Sometimes we prosper and
others, well, we move on.

Even Trek knows when
he has triumphed
because he has trained me to stop and
relish in the experience with him.

Such are the pleasures of Vermont's apples.

FIRST SNOW

The air is brisk against my skin and
portends of an early dusting of snow
as my dog, Pip, and I
stroll the logging lane leading to our home.
All around us the skeletal trees appear
silhouetted against an infinite gray sky.

I pause to absorb the majesty of
the Vermont countryside
and to marvel at
the wildlife it supports,
from the black bears who bed
in dens all winter long
to the migrating moose
who travel Vermont from top to bottom.

Just then a tiny twirling object
catches my eye:
The first snowflake of the season
steadily spirals to the ground and
slowly dissolves.

No sooner is the first gone
than others rapidly follow,
gradually starting to adhere to the road,
causing Pip and me to more leisurely
make our way home,
leaving behind us
the footprints of where we have been.

Yes, we always leave our stamp,
sometimes with little regard
as to what impact that mark has on others.
The notion may not be there long,
but it is made nonetheless;
an impression of who and what

we are and were.

And there beside my own
are Pip's paw prints; and
the loving impression he places on my life
is yet again revealed to me.

Such are the pleasures of a Vermont snow fall.

A STEALTH FOX

The weather prediction is for an
early frost. I'm enjoying a glass of wine with
my dog, Trek, red for me and air for him, out on the
terrace while the cool dusk tiptoes in
like a daddy-long-legs spider.

Trek stirs and fixes his sight on an object
moving furtively across the freshly cut
hay field. It is a stealth red fox tentatively
progressing over the drying hay inquiring for a meal.

Pausing then sniffing following a few steps,
stopping then pouncing when a morsel is revealed,
pilfering then scrutinizing his immediate environment,
preparing then prancing as he steals silently on his way.

The premature autumn evening is advancing, my
wine is quickly evaporating, and the vibrant
colors of the season are initiating their delicate dance.

A subtle joy shared with my best friend while
dinner slowly steeps in a sun-warmed, stone house.

Oh, the pleasures of a Vermont evening.

GREEN MOUNTAINS

The stature and steepness of Vermont's hills and heaps are succulently savored by my dogs, Trek and Pip, and me. Having once heaved to heights of over a mile, these mature mounts have weathered into desirable destinations to play and stay.

When autumn cleans to its conclusion our world runs russet and gray. Once the climate curls cold we are twirled with creamy, white, feathery powder. The first buds pop, reflecting muted, autumnal colors. As quickly they explode into exciting shades of emerald and jade. Completing the cycle the warm tints of fall evolve on these knolls. Like my chin, the mountains enfold us within their earnest embrace.

As the years have receded, like the height I once reached, the implements of recreation have worn away, or been put aside for more leisurely strolls. The trails we tramp are like aged wrinkles, providing each prominence with its own, precious personality.

While we miss our friends and family far afield, we have grown to honor these historic hillocks we call home. There is a comfort known only to those, like Trek, Pip and myself, who can sit silently for hours in one another's company, knowing without the exchange of words or whimpers that we are content, life is good, we're happy to share what little time we have with each other – and with these venerable peaks.

Such are the pleasures of Vermont's Green Mountains.

HARVEST

My dog, Trek, sits patiently watching me as
I scurry about,
ensuring that the seedlings
are safe from a late frost
as the planting time of year unfolds.

I plow the vegetable patch with a
neighbor's tiller, borrowed after a casual exchange
where one is mentioned as being needed.

It's with the assistance of neighbors
and acquaintances
that gardens,
both edible and not,
are sustained.

There are times these same people spot me
in the plot and stop to chew the fat.
Soon they are beside me weeding and
admiring, like the bees,
the flowers that each plant displays which will
provide the desired nourishment.

All summer we chat about the progress,
anticipating the precise moment to
pick and pluck; for the Vermont harvest suddenly
arrives with an overabundance of wealth
such that we are all sated,
for a little while.

Beginning with the prepping for planting
through to the harvest
we are aided by others.
These same people
share in each successive bounty.

The getting of help and
the giving of produce
also harvests friendships along the way.
Friends who,
while not put up or canned,
remain fresh and true.

Such are the pleasures of a Vermont harvest.

HAY

Winter rotates into spring as the air is flooded with the
gurgle from the grass as each blade stirs, stretches
and sings, soaking in the revitalizing rain while
wallowing in the warmth from the sun.

Frost heaves birth boulders, a native invasive. My dog,
Trek, and I mark their insidious presence to guard
against damage when the hay is harvested.
At ten, 60 dog years, Trek still
imagines he can catch a butterfly or
bird. Nearly the same age, I strive to keep
ahead of those things that might like to catch me.

Twice each summer a local farmer and helping hands
cut our fields. We listen for the purr of each pass
while the grass pleats in designer patterns.
The drying deepens with the fading
of the morning's dew. Raked
into rows the baling
begins. On the
beds of trucks
an amazing
number of rectangles sashay away.

Wild animals – fox and coyote – venture into the fresh
clearings, while others – hawks and owls – circle
overhead or patiently perch to sight slight
movements in the short stubble.

It is the warmth and wet of
spring and summer that
defines the time
to harvest,
and extends into a strategic
dance around afternoon thunderstorms.
The pungent scent

permeating Vermont after each cutting is
like a fresh fragrance from a
graceful hay bouquet, as
if the entire state
is going to
a ball.

Such
are the
pleasures
from hay in
Vermont.

HUMMINGBIRDS

                              May
                           is the
                          month
                     poppies bloom;
               and when a recurring whirl
         causes my dog, Trek's, ears to twitch, and my
      head to twist towards the trill. Floating fixed, staring
sideways, saluting us throughout this temperate term – we
      smile a warm welcome – our hummers have returned.

Distinguished
              by golden
                        emerald temples
                                    and jade
            crowns with dark notched tails,
         our resident male sports a distinctive
         crimson throat tipped by an ebony chin.
       Accurate angels of sunbeams polishing his
              neck radiate radiant rubies.

       The flora's scarlet color attracts his attention,
   yet the miniscule quantity of sugary nectar is what he
      requires, hovering at 70 wing whisks a second:
                   A tremendous force
                     by a tiny frame
                  for such trivial fare.

       Our solitary hummer vigorously defends the
    blossoms within his boundary. Trek's head swings left,
        right, left, while our hummer hounds intruders. A
      valiant Knight of the Roundtable, his chase chatter
             saturates the air as he jousts with his
    extended bill, his clashes like the crash of javelins.

       Akin to our heroic hummers, Vermonters always
        answer the call to protect our homeland. We are

proud of those who respond, and pay tribute to the
ones who never return, unlike the
poppies — and hummers — each May.

Such are the honorable
pleasures of our
hummers' return to Vermont.

ICE STORMS

Freezing drizzle jingles and jangles clutches and
appends; miniature sparkles alighting to delight; beaming
ice glimmers and glistens. Rays of the rising sun
reveal a multitude of miniature dazzling rainbows that
dance and gyrate decorating the view. Vibrant and
flush with spangles sequins and baubles,
Vermont has been thrillingly transformed into a
Swarovski crystal.

Early morning breezes create a cacophony of wind
chimes, coated branches swing and sway,
clinking and clattering, radiating dissonant rhapsodies.
Garlanded birch bow from the glitter's weight; evergreens
shimmer from flecks reflecting the sheen.

The frozen drips dangle –
from roofs, barns, covered bridges,
fence-rails, mustaches, fur, forests –
and flicker as the day- car- and flash- lights
echo and bounce in abundance.

Glowing off distant western frosted hills
a sliver of
luminescence explodes into copper colored
mica mirroring the rising sun, while the gel enveloped
trees to the east glint against the rosy-orange skies.

Warming, the dribbles twinkle and
shine as they thin and extend, then
charge through the air. The icicles, long
and short, snap and cascade, joining
others, dusting the ground
with effervescence. These
transient impressions
of branches, needles, wintering leaves
appear as trinkets, charms and coins,

remnants of a recent celebration.

Awakening, the radiant dawn
diminishes the gleam and
dashes the dapple until all that
remains are the
splashes to feed the unfolding spring.

Such are the pleasures
from ice storms here in Vermont.

IRENE

A tranquil beginning
with elements forging a
godhead – an arc – a swath
cut through lands longing to
dance with you. A virgin possessing gale
force headwinds sweeping far-and-wide like a
ruffled comprehensive skirt sashaying across the ballroom.

one, two, three, two, one

While we sleep you creep
closer; I wake to my dog, Trek's,
whimpers, and you knocking on our door,
bowing our trees, slashing our windows with your copious cries.
These moans swell our creeks, streams
and rivers; flooding our villages, homes, businesses;
changing the course of lives like our covered
bridges which break – twigs in your grasp,
floating beside
pieces of broken dreams.

The destruction and devastation you
fling freely
within your influence
bring tears to our eyes.
Naked and in chains
you molest and force us
to wish we could burn you alive
or, at the least, shoot an arrow through
your throat. But no martyrdom
for you as we possess the
scriptures –
hope, love, charity.

Gasping upon first sight,
recognition –

Trek provides a semblance of stability
during a time of confusion and
recovery – laughter in tears, which we dry
quickly, and pitch in to help
neighbors, friends, strangers toward a common goal. Yes,
the pleasure from you, dearest Irene,
comes from what we make of your unsolicited gifts.

During the bluest of azure skies, we unite in
peace to rebuild, resurrect, rejoice.

Such are the
pleasures
of the post-Irene Phoenix
in Vermont.

Irene: Greek goddess of Peace
Saint Irene: One of three sisters martyred for her faith (for possessing the scriptures) in 4thC Macedonia; sent to a house of prostitution, unmolested after being exposed naked and chained, she was either burned alive or shot through the throat with an arrow.

FORESTS

Like two lovers slow dancing rhythmically, our land
syncopates within a symphony: An allegro once
carpeted with lush forests, then an adagio
predominately cleared, and now a
scherzo thrust back into woods,
making for a topsy-turvy
wildlife world.

Out among the trees with my dog, Trek, we happen upon
an opus in the canopy; a jarring micro-burst fashioned
crowns dangling like unstrung strings or scattered
round the ground like busted instruments. A
chance, perhaps, for a new composition, a
masterpiece: Initiate reforestation; renew
the life-cycle; and sustain sundry
forms of flora and fauna.

Trek and I help with the
noting of trees, while others
tune landings, skid rows, water-bars.
Winter arrives securing a concerto of frozen
ground. The logging involves felling, removing,
bucking and trucking: All to benefit the wonder of nature.

What was first perceived
as a flaw of the natural world,
we exchange for scenic surroundings.
As notes become music, logs are transformed
into timber, household heat and functional furniture.

Such are the symphonic
pleasures found
in Vermont's forests.

MAPLE SUGAR

Late winter's tepid days and freezing evenings spawn the
sap's ascent from maple trees continuing a cycle from
ground to table – from yesteryear to today –
a journey of toil and time and delight.

Eastern Woodland Indians scored trunks and
trapped sap in hollowed logs; early
tintypes exemplify expansion with wooden
buckets and tanks on toboggans; more recently
metal pails appeared – rusted ones my dog, Trek, and I
discover while wandering in a
grove of wolf maples.

Plastic tubing like drunken spider patterns appear
today within the sugarbush. Hoses hand humid fluid to
electrified vessels consecutively conveyed to
evaporators for boiling. The
result: thick, sweet essence, perfect for our
visiting friends' breakfast of flavored bacon and
syrup smothered pancakes, while Trek's
company receives maple tasting treats.

Early Colonial commerce produced sugar
products. Freed from foreign sweets helped herald our
independence. We stand proud that the sweat of slaves
never stained our maple sugar.

Albeit small, sugaring played a part in our freedom, and
represents Vermonters' taste for a host of freedoms.

Such are winter's maple sugar pleasures.

MONARCH BUTTERFLIES

Hours of blacktop; hypnotic white lines;
whipping windshield wipers; telephone poles
repeating; commuting all winter to ski; and year-round
simply to sleep under an affectionately enveloping quilt of
Vermont stars.

Bushed from the back-and-forth,
my dogs, Pip and Trek, and I breathe
here fulltime. Our cottage garden, a cornucopia
of multi-colored flowers, is the focus of frequent fauna.
Magnificent monarchs, living ephemeral lives of scarcely
five weeks, grant agreeable enchantment as they alight each
spring on our delightful blossoms and blooms.

A single "Methuselah" strain,
arriving at summer's end, survives
eight months. They flit and flutter in our
garden; to Mexico migrate, hibernate, mate;
and return to reproduce in the United States. They
journey forth-and-back much as once Pip, Trek and I
did, and countless others still do.

Autumn air cools as shadows
silently stretch. We sit on our porch,
me slowly swaying, Pip patiently snoozing
and Trek tolerantly watching, as they flicker from
flower to flower, eventually landing on their namesake,
butterfly, bushes. Our exhausting roundtrips have
ended while theirs is now beginning, yet our past
practice pales in comparison to these
mighty Methuselah butterflies.

Such are the pleasures of monarchs passing thru Vermont.

MOOSE

A multitude of mammoth moose meandered freely within
fertile forests an eon prior to hard won fields framed by
stoic stonewalls interrupted their migration. Their
incidence improved with the recent enfolding of
margins and reforestation of meadows.

My dogs, Trek and Pip, and I site our first as we
cautiously maneuver the Oxbow curve. A young buck,
alone, without a rack. Assure of himself as if he were
more aged and wiser. He neither looks our way nor
acknowledges our presence, or the other
folk who stop and stare.

Related revelations abound around our abode: Hoof
marks in the mud and snow; tidbits they deposit
and desert. But we have yet to glimpse one close to home.
Second and third viewings are on the east then west sides
of Andover Ridge. Traveling solo, like the other, these
two exhibit confidence, as did our first.

Our current contacts, a female, heavier than a horse, and
her pony-sized twins, feed in a spring-fed stream. Like
others we have seen, these calves and cow are
certain of themselves. We wait in our car and watch
from a distance. A mother moose is a confrontational
champion of her children. Before we drive away,
I glance back at my dogs. Trek smiles and
Pip stares letting me know they would
assuredly like to get out and play.
But not today.

Such are the pleasures of moose sightings in Vermont!

MUD SEASON

Silent, sluggish, softening,
syncopation of snow and ice
leech below the frost and gift a
malleable, musty, mushy, mocha
season. When we had thought
hot-chocolate days were
behind us, we find travel
smothered in varieties
smooth, chunky,
thick, runny.

Alternating days consistently creamy, causing
                cautious comings and goings; different days
gooey and soggy, splattering sedans in
                      beige shades of coffee with dapples of
rainbow tints, like baby chicks, peeping through.

Car tread tracks provide dramatic
impressions of long, wind-swept, wavy,
brunette hair, flowing graceful and silky along paved roads.
                                Yet winter longs to maintain its
                    grasp with a far too brief, fragile dusting.
Two too delicate beauties and heralds of things to come.

Infrequently I
inadvertently step within the brawny
cappuccino, while my dogs, Trek and Pip, appear to
purposefully paint their paws in pathways to print
patterns of auburn flowers ornamenting
our floors and fitted carpets.

The timid travel to diverse domains where dirt is
dry and dusty, unlike our vibrant, hopeful, tan terrain,
where children of those who remain relish in the mire and
muck of mouth-watering mud-pies.

Existing within this russet season instills an appreciation
for the exquisiteness that is hiding immediately
beneath cinnamon, cardamom, ginger ground.
Subtly stirring; absolutely absorbing;
and bountifully budding, soon the
colors of spring burst forth and
coat our lives with bliss.

Such are the pleasures
from – surviving –
mud season in Vermont.

OWLS

The sun silently slips behind red, orange and
golden trees. My dog, Trek, and I depart into the
descending duvet dusk. We disregard what strength of
surveillance may be upon us as we ascend our
drive. Approaching the conclusion we reduce
momentum and are captivated by bright-golden
eyes staring out from a hefty, cream-colored,
egg-shaped form – a Snowy Owl.

Perched two feet from branch to top of head; light,
nearly white; an oversized oval-shape
heightened by the shortage of protruding ears.
Piercing yellow eyes dart from Trek to me and back
like a metronome. We are stunned to
spot such a surprising specter.

It likely wonders when we will withdraw and remove the
rumbling motor and crunching tires which are surely
frightening delicacies that might happen across
our drive and fields, filled as they are with
abundant appetizing morsels to be had simply by
stealthily surveying from its present position.
Trek and I delight in not being included in its diet.

This glimpse of an infrequent visitor brings smiles to
our faces each time we hear the hoot of a dark eyed
Barred Owl, or Eastern Screech-Owl, our
more common, local varieties.

Such are the pleasures of owl
spotting, and hearing, in
Vermont.

PORCUPINE

While an expansive feast
for our expectant guests
succulently steeps
the twilight ascends promptly
like a bedspread relaxing
into a feathered mattress. An oversized
buttery orb scales the distant hills
from underneath the
mantle, with an accompanying
evening breeze
wafting through our windows
as if a tonic.

Out the window I entertain
my agitated dog,
Trek,
using first one paw,
then the other,
to claw at his face which is,
regrettably,
pierced with porcupine quills.
While Native Americans
used these quills to make ornaments,
Trek is not bejeweled
but frightened with whiskers on end.

Solitary rodents,
porcupines feed on vegetation
and tree bark,
so Trek was not
the porcupine's intended dinner;
but Trek must have thought the porcupine looked
like a tasty morsel of licorice sticks.

These were porcupette quills,
some no more than an

inch
in length, designed to release when they
come in
contact with another animal.
They have barbs which
force the quill to work its way inside,
becoming lethal
when piercing
a major organ.

Trek encroached
on the porcupine's territory,
and certainly heard
the porcupette's shrill screeches,
whines, groans, and unfriendly chatter.
Now we
were to infringe on our
vet's evening with 40 more quills
needing removal
after the 15
we extracted
from his cheeks and lips.
No,
Trek would not
let us intrude inside his mouth.

Upon our belated homecoming
we delightfully discover
that our vacationing acquaintances
have pleasantly established
themselves after savoring their
salacious supper.
These valued friends are not
trespassing,
but are graciously welcome.

It's most agreeable
to acknowledge

that we possess such
familiar visitors aware that they
may disembark and depart at their leisure,
as well as at ours.
If only
Trek's visitations in the woods
were as welcome.

We find
such unexpected pleasures
in Vermont
prodded on by porcupines.

SNOWSHOEING

Searching, sniffing, stopping, staring, starting are our
dogs, Trek and Pip, as we shadow on snowshoes. On this
animated day we rendezvous with special
friends and their pets,
Alfie and Martha, Stuart and Nadine.

Today's energetic excursion offers the exhilaration of
continuous climbs; the treat of trampling novel trails; the
indulgence in exploring previously unfamiliar pathways; and
the bliss of brief breathers dubbed,
'taking in the view.'

As we create our marks, so too are the tracks of
personalities present in the powder:
characteristic bird claws;
indentations of towed tails of miniscule mice;
elongated heart-shaped stamps
from deer and moose hooves; and
enigmatic grooves perhaps of bear or boy.

Snowshoeing affords us the delight of deep drifts;
the freshness of frosty air;
the determination to diligently advance;
and the sparkle of eyes with faces upturned.
Our faithful friends frolic among themselves,
cheering each other,
just as we encourage one another.

Approaching the final foot
we surface in single file,
as our canine companions chase in our compact course,
affording them a soothing stroll.
The last half mile we trudge across
the pond's dam and hike up the hill to the house.
This concluding incline is
the most challenging yet ever so gratifying.

The endeavor results in treats and drinks for our entire
entourage, including shared laughter, followed by
festive food; a rejuvenating shower; and a cozy
fire. Ah, the steal from a spirited mission.
We will sleep deeply from the exertion.

Such are the pleasures of snowshoeing
in Vermont.

SNOWSHOE HARE

On a clear spring morning driving home
from Londonderry
my dog, Trek, while hanging out the window,
spots a snowshoe hare bounding across our path.

The hare possesses incredibly visible, huge
hind feet; it is these same rear feet that rocket him
out-of-sight. All the while Trek leaps
from window-to-window,
but the snowshoe hare vanishes in
an instant.

This is no ordinary bunny for
his size indicates he could have been
the Mad Hatter late for a very important date.
But instead of a pocket watch, top hat and tails, he
is clothed in the markings of the season – a dreary gray.

But each winter, like a Chameleon,
he becomes completely white
to blend in with the snow. His back feet
are enormously outsized to carry him across the
cover during daily jaunts to secure food. Being
white against the snow protects him from
many predators, but not all. Yes, like other wild creatures,
he is part of the food chain in the Vermont woods.

And like other bunnies
he breeds
numerous times a year.
Endurance in the wild is the nature of the game,
and this guy does well for himself and
for others; for it is during the winter
that we think of his serving
more as a food source for the feral
carnivores, yet one more survival mechanism.

Yes, it is the arrangement of the Universe
that all things have their time and place. The
hare is here for a purpose
— as Trek is my companion
— we are all present for one another
— in one form or another.

Such are
the pleasures
of being a hare here
in Vermont.

SUNRISE

Awakened just before dawn
by the requests of my dog, Trek,
we silently journey into the fresh,
shadowless atmosphere.

Walking westerly we are unaware
of the transformation taking place.
But as we turn to face east
the majesty of the morning materializes.

The distant dale is hidden
by a sea of slow moving fog.
The tops of the isolated hills
begin to surface like islands.

Across the horizon is a swath of sky
with a compilation of clouds sitting above.
As the strip of sky grows lighter,
the bottom of the collection of clouds
begins to take on, at first, a subtle tint of red/orange,
which, as Trek and I make our way closer to home,
becomes more vibrant
until the clouds appear to be ablaze.

Reveling in this sight,
feeling tipsy with joy,
we stop to admire this wonder of nature,
as a hawk flies over towards the fire in the sky.
We watch as it alights on the top of a tree,
a silhouette against the brightening sliver of sky.
Abruptly the vibrant sun explodes into view
precisely where the hawk has lit.
We stand in awe
watching the sun engulf the tree and hawk.

Without warning there arises a Phoenix,

waving its wings, wrestling to be resurrected.

No longer able to look
in the direction of the blinding orange orb,
I turn smiling towards Trek and
notice he, too, is smiling at me.

Forever more this site will be relived
in my mind's eye with the birth of each day.

Such are the pleasures of a Vermont sunrise.

THUNDERSTORMS

Until recently my dogs,
Trek and Pip,
had not cowered from thunder or
lightening,
but as the years have revolved
like cumulus clouds,
they now cower at my side,
shivering
when the crackle
and
clap
from the cosmos commences.
It is comforting for me as well,
their leaning on me,
grounding the three of us.

The forecast calls for a severe thunderstorm.
Arrive it does,
exactly as calculated;
both Trek and Pip appear trembling at my feet
right on schedule.
Reaching down to reassure
I stroke their heads. They meekly peek up,
quivering, probing my eyes for encouragement.
I smile at them
even though I know they won't smile back.

The windows rattle
from the wind,
that shifts the deluge diagonally
yet virtually in a straight line.
As it traverses our property
the drenching strafes the dry soil.
I call to worn a friend
that the column of rain
will soon knock at her door.

As the storm recedes,
the ever enriching sun emerges
causing the remnants of rain
to twinkle like shards of glass sparklers
celebrating the conclusion of the storm.
Rapidly
a radiant rainbow encloses these glimmering lights.
As my eyes
slide along the multi-colors,
they alight at the terminus
that is surrounding my neighbor's home.

Ecstatically reflecting on the stunning site,
I phone to enlighten her
that she is the completion
of one of the most celebrated color festivals
of the summer.
And she, in turn,
notifies me
that at that very moment
Trek, Pip and I
are at the beginning of the formation
of one of the most brilliant spectrums
she has ever seen

Here in Vermont
we are all,
at one time or another,
the anchors for one end,
or the other,
of all the dazzling rainbows
assigned to us
by thunderstorms.
At different times
we are the recipients
of the arc flowing so gracefully overhead,
blessing us,

protecting us,
like Trek and Pip are for me,
and I for them.

Such
are
the pleasures
of thunderstorms
here
in
Vermont.

TURKEYS

Birth of buds
and blooms
bordering forests
builds autumnal colors
to initiate spring. Break-of-dawn
earthly masqueraders tote tools to
proffer a gobbler, the tom.
Human hunters
crossing our yard
are unlike
my dog, Trek, and I
who seldom seek turkeys
or their groups
that gorge at grub in the grass.

With nearly 360° sight, they
study the surroundings for strangers.
When seen they vocalize a warning of any
and all possible predatory presence:
Like the huntsmen, Trek, or me.

Unexpectedly
we witness a tom,
with tail in full flush,
strutting his stuff.
Apparently
little interest is shown,
yet he continues his quest.
Head of a harem – in his mind only – toms travel
with other gobblers and older jakes:
A bunch of bachelors.

During May
the hens sit and lay.
Akin to humans who during maternity
talk and sing to their young;

hens communicate with their brood
while still encased
within the
shells.
Before long they travel forth
from forests to fields
with their poults, both jennies
and jakes; and the clucks continue
with commands to come
back, scatter, hide.

Thanks to an abundance of wild turkeys,
as in a Norman Rockwell painting,
our dining room table's
a Thanksgiving feast spread for family,
friends,
and "orphans"
– those missing relations
with whom to share
the holiday.

Such are the pleasures of turkeys,
especially during November,
in Vermont.

TURTLES

Sustained
by forested field
fairies, succulent
springs supply
three
ponds near
our home. Each pool spills over into successively superior
sizes, shaping the stream that runs beside the road
nearby.
Water bodies are wonderful
winter dwellings for turtles whose skin,
by magician's magic, absorbs oxygen from water.

Sun's dappled daylight dawns through dimpled clouds on
the summer morning my dog, Trek, and I meet a turtle tirelessly
attempting to traverse the road. Although sage, having arisen from
an ancient assembly of animals, they lack common sense, like this one
requiring assistance on its travels.

In the spring they stay close to wet spaces, gradually
moving farther to forage and lay their eggs, returning to wetlands to
breed and winter. While they may live 60 years, their survival is
wobbly: Humans being their major hazard. But today we
pose no threat as we help our friend securely cross
the asphalt and return home.

Trek and I
don't live in a dog house, but in one made
of stone. And turtles don't live in their
sculpted shells, but in wetlands,
wood-lands and meadows.
And while
Trek, or I for that matter, may not live as long as they, we
are happy to share what we have as long
as
we
may.

Such are the pleasures turtles transport throughout Vermont.

SEASONS OF VERMONT

Varied are the expressively named flavors visiting our land,
excessively masquerading or momentarily materializing.

I.   Winter
Seemingly everlasting, crossing year-to-year: Bleak, arctic, cyclic
white wind –
        wintry white –
                wind wintry –
                        white wintry wind....

Delicate descending snow – swish, swoosh, crunch – burning
wood, steaming cider – prickling cold, invigorating warmth:
Totality results in tolerably tasty, comfy cozy, minimally
minuscule days with prolonged nights – ever so dry
while ever so wet.

II.   Sugaring
Requisite February thaw launches smoke signals billowing from
sugarhouses: Folks drop-in to ensure neighbors endure the
                      white wind –
              wintry white –
        wind wintry –
white wintry wind...

and to share Myrrha's ambrosia: Distilled maple syrup with
a shot of whisky – fortification till Boreas succumbs.

III.   Mud
Rigid, relentless snow gradually loosens its frigid fascination,
tingling the obscure, dormant desire as March expires and the
mucky month of April beckons. A pristine white gown draping
mountainsides slips silently, softly, like silk, revealing the
virgin season veiled by bare yet bud-filled boughs.

Persephone hurrying home, with an occasional, fleeting look
behind. Snowdrop patches poke through trumpeting her return,

simply to be covered by a glance back, another pasty blizzard.

Ducks stealthily arrive in supportive pairs following the sun on its measured rotation from horizon to tree tops and beyond; deer, bear, moose, fox – wondrous wildlife – emerge with newborn, adding to the transformation, majesty and marvel.

Not yet stored, plows and shovels aid in removing a fresh fluffy fall, followed in fast procession by a successor, clinging to drooping branches, mounding on roofs and fences, burying all anxiously awaiting the sun's cloaking passion. Blusters whip clumps into minor mountain ranges with modulating peaks glistening in shafts of sunlight. Swirling flurries reflect rays, glittering in a free fall in a late frozen flash.

Confusion abounds during this commutation; a glimpse over a shoulder brings a fierce polar nor'easter, hard and harsh: Rivers overflow, dirt roads switch into thick soupy mush. Will shivering conclude and warming commence, unfolding spring like patriotic flags longing to flap from porch or pole?

Snow timidly retreats from tree trunks. Crusting motes provide precarious bridges to nowhere engulfed in randomly occurring fog. The sun's brightness breaks through unadulterated, instantly cutting a gleaming path across our flooded flower wonderland.

Feel crocus stir, rise, resist nippy nights; hear pregnant robins scratch, peck and pull at exposed patches of earth. Plowed, mounded, drifted snowfalls morph into invigorating drink for infant roots in search of nectar, exposing jaundiced tulips thirsting for the sun's synthesis, the effervescent sparkle.

Sun percolated water collects into coffee colored syrup declining into a denser chocolate as days pass, gratifying an awakening spring. Stout perennials display slight but sturdy shoots – royal tiaras. Perpetual raspberries and hardy hazelnuts inflate as if dressing for a ball with disguised flowers appended to couture.

Distant miasma – ripening tree leaves – alludes to autumn's return coloring the scenery in shades fair-haired, strawberry blond. Joie de vivre permeates April's terminus with a promising nose of bright beginnings from stimulating rain showers.

IV.   Spring

May dawns as a thin scent of defrosted dirt and heady whiffs of hyacinths – Persephone's triumphant return. Tepid days vibrate with affection; riding high the sun alights on slices previously devoid; nights shift from raw to cool, swelling successive days' zest.

On Green-Up Day love-in-idleness' likeness of Elizabethan johnny-jump-ups and pansies rule in novel vibrant variants – staggering colors – some muted deviations in tone: A rainbow of crosspollination, hues in astonishing, dainty disparity.

Beside the chill generous bumble bees work their wonder: Fruit trees blossom, blueberries chime pale. Lily bulbs' spiral stair-step waltz awakens; leggy elegant fiddleheads bubble to the top; tansy breaks through; thyme, dill, sage, parsley foliate.

Flimsy, heavy-headed poppies protrude from furry folios; hydrangea, viburnum leaf replete. Goldfinch and bluebirds frolic; barn swallows busily build a nest in a bleached birdhouse atop a split rail fence; time for toms to gobble in excess.

Rapturous replenishment!

In the youthful shade bleeding hearts sprout and drip in a row like virgin's tears; lily-of-the-valley progressively expands in a chain alongside the devoted hostas and waiting astilbe loosening their coils. It is the reign of the lilac, conveying joyous aroma that brings home hummers in fanciful flight.

Straight and stiff squirt iris, spiking the stratosphere. Lupines many fingered leaflets awaken aching for an embrace. Scatter grain harvested last fall; plant dependable annuals; resurrect window boxes for summer's spectacle.

Love's oracle, golden dandelion kings, dot the countryside as if painted by Seurat, turning emerald grass to a carotene glow. Prosperous peonies peek through in search of sun, leaving us tingling with expectation! When leopard's bane blooms in brilliant citron, and Chinese globeflower burgeons all buttery, there by the edge of the pond, a mallard with her ducklings.

Exquisite as lace poppy tissue-petals explode in oriental citrus. Caterpillars' webs loom to florets doom. Notus brings drop-after-drop; plants quiver in a dance to the everlasting love of the soil yielding brainy morel mushrooms in conical shapes.

As the lunar revolution fades away we remember our fallen on Memorial Day. There can be no doubt we honor their service as we cut our last Asparagus sprouts A chance of thunderstorms greets each day as we bring to a close the minutes of May; and materializing as if a crown a light delicate dusting of little lilac corolla carpet the ground.

V.   Black Fly

Mingling with earth's melodious moist perfume – a summer whiteout – dandelion seeds swirl as June drives home. Spurts show instantly as life's measured succession sets up in earnest. Hanging columbines unlock origami complexity in hues of cumulus, tutu and calamine; false indigo rotates rapidly up reeds promoting profuse pointillism in the luminous landscape.

Gloomy areas sorcerized by measured unfurling of foreign ferns in diverse varieties and Zen-like watercolors; burgundy coral bells flourish in shadows. Dignified dahlias stretch refreshed from a beneficial rest. Creative climbing vines weave tapestries on tête-à-tête trellis.

Our very own clover steps sprightly in its proliferation of three and – some particularly special – four leaf forms. Mammoth and Autumn Beauty strive like Icarius for the fiery orb. Muggy afternoons fetch irritating no-see-ums, black flies biting.

Irises, bearded and Siberian, extend their taffy like tufts and ethereal peddles that ruffle in the zephyr. Sweet, sweet Williams open to fizzy gloss appearing in abandon having been dispersed on wings of angels. Pincushiony knapweed and carpet bugleweed expand as if blown by the breath of god.

Vivacious, luxurious, fashion statements – azure geraniums, profusion pink prouder, shocking Venetian red dianthus – compliment subdued pastels. Ovules have begun maturing into nourishment for feathered and furry friends. Weed in earnest while swallows frantically provide for their brood, adding enchantment to our harmonious Elysium Fields.

As if yawning daisies, cone flowers parade spirited white, radiant cerulean, cheerful cherry. Black-eyed Susan and purple Vivian proliferate in scattered manifestations. Bluebell comfrey and crimson vigalia are nosh for butterflies and bees; gladiolas' solitary spires judiciously elevate. Multi-colored wildflowers erupt without discrimination – our reflection.

Fickle June projects the unexpected: The day's air scorches nostrils, but nary ruffles silvery angel hair Artemisia; an abrupt scent of rain, a cold front lifting the heavy weight from these endless days. Every blue, black and rasp-berry swells; crops engorge from daily thunderstorms, clapping, striking a crystalline proclamation. In the approaching dusk, a mass migration of fireflies slowly arises, creating a cornucopia of light to celebrate mid-summer's eve.

June's culmination nears as meadow rue's redolent pungency prickles with darts of color; yarrow effloresces into bubbles of tingling tints; and perky pink alliums prance into prime.

A profusion of penstemon's sylphlike stems open petite ruby bearded trumpets passionately craved by hummers. Canterbury bells skipped a year, make a marked manifestation with Jaipur upturned chimes; ever faithful false lupine with saffron pineal crowns render June's conclusion into a Shangri-La.

VI. Summer

Joyously July washes ashore in a blizzard of bugs. Sniff first cut hay dodging rainy days. Fledging barn swallows line a limb awaiting regurgitated insects and coaching before taking flight.

As the gunpowder smoke subsides from our nation's birth celebration, peonies proliferate. The mature growth of goat's beard fades without being trimmed; and weeding never ends.

Our reward: flamingo lady slippers; our surprise: Queen Ann's lace. Kernels mysteriously ferried create cottage gardens Monet would envy. Splashes of coreopsis and violas decorate pockets of heaven. All the while snap peas cling and ascend while squash expands into scrumptious orbs.

Beside evening primrose's shiny cups, clematis clambers around an abandoned horse drawn plow; substantial lapis lazuli blossoms spread like patchwork covering the rusty iron.

Masked Marguerite's minute daisy mustard dots and fernlike foliage prospers from prior scattering. Milfoil spreads in pastel coral, heliotrope, robin egg, and buttermilk. Spiderwort spears and dangles white or mauve chambers that daily open then lock. Mango, margarine daylilies abound along roads, stone walls.

Spreading the wealth Lucifer crocosmia stabs aloft with perfectly aligned vermillion trumpets, broadcasting as July rounds the bend. Nature constructs as it also destructs.

Yet life continues revived, rewarded. Picture delphinium – midnight blue, pink sensation, spotted bluebird, magic fountain – gallantly reaching new heights, caressing the sky. Navigate Eden's paths; absorb pungent prized potpourri of lavender.

Sturdy stalks of sunflowers kiss the ether, foresee a copious heyday. Phlox pop in tones of sapphire, electric maraschino, magenta, and keys in-between; variegated blanket flowers sally out in striations of saffron, mandarin and carmine. Wild white and aqua marine mallows entertain; minty bee balm in carnelian and fandango boogie, magnetize flying friends.

Six-foot goldenquelle canes climax in canary; scabiosa pincushion in ankle high robin-egg, waist height rich beet, and sun-drops towering on seven foot shafts: Dizzying delicacies. The apex: A cacophony of color.

July perishes with overbearing heat, causing one to wonder why
                                      white wind –
                wintry white –
was ever a bother. Life takes note and prophesies a protracted slumber. Days get shorter; mums and wildlife respond.

VII.   Harvest

Heavy, humid air of August arrives on a tropical blast singing a hallowed hymn of prosperity: Joyous fruition and profusion! Scarecrows surface to farmer's dismay, ebony crows' delight.

Rose, creamy-gilt, bisque, maroon abutting stark white with freckles: Lily blooms persist in providing a prevailing perfume. Mutated cone-flower-bee-balm plum-topped, daisy-like blossoms afford a sense of awe. Life is amazing yet transient.

Inundated overnight: Love-apples; slender, tender haricot vert; pocket-sized potatoes; fleshy zucchini; still snapping peas; and latticed filigree of challenging cross-word puzzles – carrot tops. Corn's sculpted cobs egotistically spray silk like overflowing Parisian fountains. Beet greens evoke deep emerald, rouge.

Powdery blueberries enliven pancakes, pies; frozen cobalt spheres supply memories of bounteous days. Finishing phlox flare into utopian palettes of whitest whites, scarletest scarlets, fuchsiaest fuchsias. Volleying one-by-one gossamer gladiola rungs yield insignia in notes of peach, milk, pepper, honeydew.

Feel the exuberant dahlias, statuesque in their deep persimmon, garnet, bronze, apricot, and amethyst. Listen as the orchestra's warm-up synchronizes into a symphony worthy of Brahms.

Vermont brims as the blazing flora dance and sway in delirium with the wind as their partner. Butterfly bushes' essence ruptures joining others whose soul, if lucky, will proffer splendorous excess in parts previously stripped of substance.

An arctic salvo greets late August. Fruit trees drop their yield – sustenance to all wanderers. Shadows lengthen as dogs roam across the room in search of the progressing sunny spots.

Days may miss seventy; nights lower into the forties. The sturgeon moon waxes ahead of a premature rime. Ah, the rain comes cooler, when it comes. Having begun so lusciously lilies are all but faded memories, and so, August folds away.

VIII. Canning

September's bracing breeze bends before a ruffling reminder; consecutive sun downs shed significant heat and light.

Prodigious provisions – continuous harvesting – an abundance of lean, crisp beans; sexy delectable, amazing acidic tomatoes and mellow corn. Soccer and beach ball-sized pumpkins allude that soon they will rally into the safety zone.

Days alternate between toasty and chilly. Apple's spice infuses kitchens with beckoning choruses. Time to heed the whispers: "Beware the full moon," "hurry and harvest." The first faint frost lies in silver and green streaks across the field vaguely freezing the morning dew, awaiting the call.

Fragile cosmos, blooming late, luxuriates in a restrained elfin rainbow like the poppies that initiate rotation. Multi-pedaled, season's suffix-celebrations amaze with rejuvenating, painted spires. Borrowed seeds purposely placed where their blush will be cherished in subsequent spells; others saved for unknown areas emptied by the oncoming winter's fallen comrades.

Pansies pantomime; black-eyed Susan persists; coreopsis peaks in Chantilly ivory, hints of orange sherbet; lavender exhales mauve incense. Spiderwort spreads webs on legs of concord-grape and snow-white. Gaillardia blankets of kumquat and amber turn to feathery progeny whisked afar.

Towering seven feet Jerusalem artichokes loll, bask, wave in fervent colors; suspended saucers donate succulent nectar. Swamp maples turn radish and tangerine as the second cutting of hay permeates the air.

Final finials, penultimate penstemon, and belated butterfly bushes: Honeyed fragrance for migrating monarchs. Animated asters and charged chrysanthemums exhibit amethyst starburst variations; tansy's turmeric poke-a-dots tango atop fragile ferns; dianthus dance in crimson crowns; modified iris leaves pirouette to a pulsating painter's pallet.

Days disappear as Persephone journeys asunder, sweeping in a storm to deliver a maiden's bitter attack. September's ending is clear, brisk with wisps of cirrus floating in a turquoise sky, conveying a glacial covering to lull the plants into a trance.

Unwinding, listening to the approaching nippy evening, wanting not to bundle but in wishing to watch an added layer of human mulch, a sweater, is required. So quiet, yet so busy as animals forage and grow fat storing for winter.

IX.   Foliage

Boreas forces October home on cold, wet, gray clouds portending an untimely arrival. Temperatures plummet, skies crystalline, the smell of organic compost permeates the air.

Changing from pleasant emerald to hearty bullion – even fiery ginger – some when wet glimmer violet, vivid leaves flutter in spiraling sails like dancing emblems, as trees sway in rhythm.

Onerous tempests split spindles, supplying cuttings for vases. Tubers are rescued, vegetation wilts below skeletal, straw maize rustling in the bluster. Hoary nights, bleak days present a constant challenge. Indian summer teases, creating a forged optimism that the final fretful icy covering may never appear. Yet come it must, turning life giving foliage into mush.

Rush, reap pumpkins, melons; cut sage, thyme, parsley, basil and hang to dry; transport ruddy rosemary indoors.

Once discarded our vivacious maple, fir, ash, beech logos dot the ground like confetti – rustle, crackle, dazzle under foot. Tourists are enchanted even when wicked gales capture the vistas, stealing our auburn, burgundy and carroty charms.

Hummers depart leaving other migrants to pluck hanging sunflower husks. Their songs denote storing window boxes; pruning fruit trees; cleaning and covering stalwart perennials. We buttress against a cold onslaught, Persephone's absence.

Sunrise sees rust and umber trees secreting a wine-colored hue, an autumn bouquet, undercurrents of spring growth. Aerated vines rotate into thick blood like exposed cells of naked limbs.

Ah, pumpkins pop in strategic places to ward off evil.

Midas touched tamarack needles drop, decorating hillsides for a last dab of color. Relics remaining at tops of oaks and aspens shimmer, sound a light twinkling, travel like strands of reddish-brown and fair-haired fog across forest tops.

October's closing days are loaded with hibernacula activity. Inhale night air of sugary smoldering wood. Lashing squalls put a period on the month, hammering rain and corpulent snow distributing needed moisture for the interminable winter.

X.   T'aint Nothin'
Passing into November milkweed pods shoot stars on gusts
foreshadowing vast snowfalls.

The in-between time:
trees blown bare display sticks and twigs;
ground turns brownish gray exposing stones.

A time we find ourselves alone – together.

Acknowledgements

I would like to thank The Old Parish Church in Weston, Vermont for previously publishing on their website "Butterflies in Love." I would also like to thank a group of poets in Andover, Vermont who allowed me to bring several of these poems to their meetings (Betty Hord Edelman, Bruce Hesselbach, Timothy Swaim Johnson, Susan Lieder, Anne Mausolff). I appreciate their guidance.

I also owe gratitude to Vermont Coverts: Woodlands for Wildlife, a nonprofit organization which was instrumental in my education of the wonders of the woods and wildlife found in Vermont.

I owe much gratitude to both Jane Sarly and Fiona Morton for their listening, reading and editing skills; and to Liz Steger for her help creating the cover art and both Martha Bartsch and Marc Hartzman for their cover design advice.

Lastly, I'd like to thank my family, without whom I would never have been able to begin this journey. Especially my dogs, Trek and Pip, who helped me see things in this world through their eyes. My life would have been less than had they not been a part of it.

Made in the USA
Charleston, SC
27 February 2013